# George Best

IRIS HOWDEN

GW00702884

If you like football,
you probably have a favourite player.

For some it was Pele, or Maradona,
for others it was Jimmy Greaves.

Now it may be Gazza.

One player stands out above them all.
He seems to sum up
what football is all about.

That man is George Best.

There is a story
about the manager of Manchester United,
Sir Matt Busby.
He gave his team the same team-talk
every week before the match.

"If you want to win this match,"
he said,
"every time you get the ball –
just pass it to George Best."

As a player he was simply the best.
He was called a genius
or an artist.
He was a joy to watch.

He had ball control.
He had balance.
Most of all he had speed.
He could go from standing still
to full speed in a split second.

# The Early Years

George Best was born on May 22nd 1946.
He grew up
on a big working class housing estate
just outside Belfast.

As a boy he lived for football.
He played in the school team
and for the local youth club.

He spent hours working on his skills.
He would kick a tennis ball
against a kerb or a garage door.

He was a small and skinny boy.
The only way to beat the bigger boys
was to run faster than them.

One day, a scout for Manchester United
came to watch a youth match
that Best was playing in.

He sent a message to the manager
Sir Matt Busby.

It said:
"I think I have found a genius."

Best joined the club at 15
– but he nearly blew his big chance.

He got so homesick,
he went back to Belfast
after just two days.

His dad made him change his mind
and try again.
It was lucky for George Best,
and lucky for the world of football!

# Manchester United

Best played his first match
for Manchester United first team
in September 1963.

In 1964
he got his first cap for Northern Ireland,
a month before his 18th birthday.

In those days,
Manchester United was trying
to build a new team.
Many of its best players had been killed
in the famous air crash at Munich.

Best was one of the new "Busby Babes".
Everyone could see
the glory days would soon be back.

# Glory Days

In 1965,
Best's first full season with the club,
United won the League title.

Next year they got to the semi-final
of the European Cup.

In the quarter-final,
they had played Benfica of Portugal.

Benfica were a strong side,
and Sir Matt told his team
to play safe
at the start of the match.

Best did not seem to hear this advice.
He scored twice in the first 12 minutes!

In the European Cup semi-final
next season,
Best scored one goal
and set up another
to beat Real Madrid of Spain.

In the final,
Manchester United played Benfica again.

Best scored to give United a 1-0 lead.
Then Benfica scored,
and the game went to extra time.

Then, in the first minute of extra time,
Best got the ball.
He beat his man near the half way line,
ran up field,
stepped round the goalkeeper
and slid the ball into the net.

He made it look so easy.

United went on to win 4-1.

They were the first English side
to win the European Cup.

This was a wonderful season
for George Best.
He was United's top goal scorer
with 28 goals.

He was voted Footballer of the Year,
then European Footballer of the Year.

# Troubles

But the good times did not last.

Because he was small and light,
Best became a target
for the hard men in football.

He was always being kicked and hacked down.
He had to put up with body checks,
shirt pulling and other professional fouls.

He couldn't always handle it.
His temper got him into trouble,
and he often got booked
because he argued with the ref.

Off the field he was just as wild.

Best was football's first pop star.
At the height of his fame,
he got 10,000 fan letters a week.

Girls threw themselves at him.
He went out with Miss World.
His picture was always on the front page.

He owned a nightclub and a boutique.
The money rolled in – and he spent it.

He bought trendy clothes and flash cars.
He was seen in every smart club.
Then he started to gamble
– and to drink.

Soon he began to miss training.

He would go drinking
for days on end.
At one point he ran away to Spain.

In the end he had a row
with United's new manager
Tommy Docherty.

Best walked out.

He played his last game for United
on 1st January 1974.

# After United

Best joined other clubs.
He went to Stockport and to Fulham.
He played for Hibs in Scotland.

He even tried to make a new life
playing football in America.

But the old Best magic
had more or less dried up.

He tried hard to get his life together.

In 1978 he married a model,
Angela MacDonald James.
They have a baby son, Calum.

But the marriage did not last.
He could not stop drinking.
In 1981 he booked into a clinic
in San Francisco to dry out.

He even tried having an implant
in his stomach
to put him off drinking alcohol.

# What Went Wrong?

Many people felt really sad
when George Best's career ended.
People still talk about the waste
of such a wonderful talent.

Some think the blame lies with him.
He admits that he got bored easily.
He had a temper that made him lash out.
He could not handle the pressures of success.

He says it was like living in a goldfish bowl.
The press followed him everywhere,
watching his every move.

There were pressures in the game too.
He could never have an off day.
Every time he played,
people expected him to score goals,
and be a "football genius".

Even today, people know Best's face.

They come up
and talk about the old days.
Some people try and tell him
where he went wrong!

In spite of it all,
Best has survived.

He can make a living as a coach,
or by playing exhibition matches.
He has worked on TV
during two World Cups.

Thanks to the video machine,
we can still enjoy seeing him in action.
The old Best magic is caught on video
for a new generation of fans.

And he is still the Best!